ARE THERE ANY BOOMERS IN HEAVEN?

P J ANDERSON

WestBow Press
A DIVISION OF THOMAS NELSON
& ZONDERVAN

Copyright © 2016 P J Anderson.

All rights reserved. No part of this book may be used or reproduced by any means, graphic, electronic, or mechanical, including photocopying, recording, taping or by any information storage retrieval system without the written permission of the author except in the case of brief quotations embodied in critical articles and reviews.

WestBow Press books may be ordered through booksellers or by contacting:

WestBow Press
A Division of Thomas Nelson & Zondervan
1663 Liberty Drive
Bloomington, IN 47403
www.westbowpress.com
1 (866) 928-1240

Because of the dynamic nature of the Internet, any web addresses or links contained in this book may have changed since publication and may no longer be valid. The views expressed in this work are solely those of the author and do not necessarily reflect the views of the publisher, and the publisher hereby disclaims any responsibility for them.

Any people depicted in stock imagery provided by Thinkstock are models, and such images are being used for illustrative purposes only. Certain stock imagery © Thinkstock.

ISBN: 978-1-5127-5620-3 (sc)
ISBN: 978-1-5127-5619-7 (e)

Library of Congress Control Number: 2016915004

Print information available on the last page.

WestBow Press rev. date: 09/15/2016

PREFACE

This may seem like an odd title for a book, but being a boomer myself and having experienced life in the church in the United States for the last thirty years or so, I think it can be a challenging question. My experience may be somewhat limited to cover such a broad topic as this, but I would like to offer a challenge to my generation to consider our impact on the church, both in the present and in the future. As a layman who has served in many roles within the church, I can probably relate to many of you who have had similar experiences, both positive and some that were not so compelling, let's say.

If you are looking for a dynamic treatise, this is definitely not it. My hope is that you can focus on some of the concerns I will address from my humble perspective, and I want to stay as close as possible to the message and examples we have been provided in the scriptures to offer some challenges to my fellow boomers. If you are looking for a fun read, this isn't it by any stretch of the imagination.

The Boomer Wave

I am sure that we all know by now that the boomer generation consists of that seventy-plus-million-people group born between the years 1946 and 1964. I am an early boomer and have had the pleasure, or not, of experiencing the many changes brought about by this unique generation. We have been labeled many things, some good and some not so good, as some have seen us as a self-oriented cultural group bringing about change in many aspects of our nation, including our own brand of what the church should look like and focus on. Now I would like to highlight some of my concerns with the church as we have influenced it to meet our needs and expectations.

v

CHAPTER 1

SOME OF MY CONCERNS

Jesus Flakes

The title of this chapter is a play on words from the "Jesus freak" movement that took place in the late sixties and early seventies. That movement was definitely part of the boomer wave. But I want to look at this from a different perspective. I am choosing to use *flakes* instead because of all the church and denominational hopping that our generation seems to have engaged in over the last thirty years or so.

Just so you don't think I am pointing fingers, my wife calls us Catho-Congo-nondenoma-Baptists. This lays out the path we traveled in our journey, coming to Christ in our thirties. We had to learn that not all teaching is biblical. I also know there are a good number of boomers who stayed true to their churches and denominations. What I am saying is that we have had a lot of movement—some of it for legitimate doctrinal issues but a lot of it related to worship formats, music choices, better preachers at a different church, and so forth. A lot of it seems a little flaky—thus the term. I have seen a lot of people come and go in the church we have been serving in for the last twenty-five-plus years. I think it is disturbing and detrimental to the advancement of the kingdom of God, which is my understanding for why the church exists in the first place.

The bottom line is this: How do you develop a ministry that can influence and serve a community, and how do you build a strong church body? How do you have the support and accountability for one another if so many in the church will leave at the drop of a hat the first time things

P J Anderson

don't go their way? Pastors have to walk on eggshells and make sure their sermons are not offensive or potentially challenging. How can the body get trained up for ministry and serve their communities faithfully? How do we fulfill the edict of reaching the world for Christ through our missionary support? How can we develop strategies that take years to develop? How do we work together to reach the generations coming behind us if most of the focus is on keeping us in the seats? Where is the spiritual growth and depth we all need to sharpen and challenge one another to attain? It all seem quite flaky to me!

Pass the Kool-Aid

My next concern is the plethora of teachings and doctrinal issues that have developed over these same years. These teachings and issues have caused much separation and disunity in the body as a whole. If you look at all the denominations and subdenominations that have come into existence, all of them claim to have the corner on truth. Throw in the nondenoms, and you have quite a theological concoction. A good number even have their own seminaries to make sure you get it right. You only need to turn on the TV to get a glimpse of what I am saying.

My concern is that I understand people can approach God from a different perspective or enjoy different worship styles, but there is only one book! How can we have so many versions of the same story? And isn't Christ at the center of that story, particularly His teachings on what is and is not important? Isn't He clear about what He wants us to focus on? Are we really so dull that we can't see through the charlatans out there peddling their health and wealth or the must-dos that have no bearing on scripture? Huge sums of money are being donated to some of these clowns, with a lot of it funding their mansions or personal needs. Some jokesters have even come along later in history to say that they need to add on to the scriptures or complete what Christ said; they've created whole new movements that millions are buying into. I will let you fill in the blanks for who I am addressing here, but I think it's obvious and unbelievable. How did we ever get here, and how will we reach future generations with such a load of unnecessary baggage and hogwash?

Relevant Worship

When we look at the variations in worship, it can almost seem comical when you hear the opinions on this. People argue about what type of musical instruments are acceptable or not! We seem to emphasize style so much, particularly as it relates to the various generations, and we have had our own wars inside the boomer movement for sure. This seems to be another one of those issues that people make major decisions about regarding where they choose to attend worship services. Seriously, should this be a primary reason for church selection or a reason for changing churches? This seems to be another one of those distractions that keeps us from centering on the important purpose and function of the church.

The Mega Movement

We have definitely been at the center of the mega movement, where the megachurches have had enormous influence on the church movements in our generation. They have enormous staffs and resources that they can provide for other churches. The problem is that most of the smaller churches can't provide the horsepower needed to mirror the megachurches, and many have fallen short and failed to measure up. They have been unable to make the program work.

A key question needs to be asked regarding this movement: Is this really the best method or model to reach our culture overall? It seems that when these big churches start moving, many other churches in that geographic area have issues as they lose attenders to the big new church in the neighborhood. How many churches do we drive by, and how many towns do we pass through to get to the right one? How many solid but small churches are closing because of lack of support and funding? Are we closing off entire communities from having a solid witness in their neighborhood? Oh, I forgot—we don't have neighborhoods in the suburbs, just fenced-off, self-contained little kingdoms called middle-class homes. Guess I answered my own question on that one! Realistically, are we building into our communities when our witness and focus is several towns away or in a city farther down the highway? Are we growing and expanding

P J Anderson

our witness within the communities in which we live? Are we purposely planting healthy churches in these communities? In the situations I have been able to experience in the developing world, the people there just don't seem to put much emphasis on buildings. They more or less go out with just the shirts on their backs to plant churches. The church in China is on foot, heading back across the old trade routes, and they will reach Jerusalem before us! It's something to think about.

One main issue relates to the use of our resources and priorities for spending. Collectively, we are the richest Christian population ever to walk the face of the earth. I daresay there will be some serious accountability regarding that in our not-too-distant future. I am willing to guess that if we took half of the money spent on buildings and related hardware, we could have produced material and sent out or partnered with indigenous groups to reach many, if not all, of the unreached that we have been clearly directed to focus our attention toward. We seem to be focused on building kingdoms down here, and as I understand it, His kingdom is not of this world. Need we go to Europe to tour the many empty cathedrals that were built to bring God glory? Many are now mere relics and museums of a previous generation's infatuation with earthly kingdom structures. They are mostly empty and void of any witness for current generations. That couldn't happen here, could it? I heard about a glass cathedral in California that is in the throes of this now—and we are only at the beginning of the receding boomer wave.

Identity Crisis

The bottom line on a lot of this, as I see it, is that we have an identity crisis in the church. It has to have our name or our brand on it to be relevant and something we will be interested in pursuing. Could you even imagine the witness we could provide in our communities if we put down our spiritual swords and worked together to reach our world for Christ? I have heard it said that on the mission field a lot of organizations have to work together to get things done. What if we approached our local community work that way? Would it make a difference? I think it would, and along with that, it would take out some of the false pride and haughtiness that only set us

Are There Any Boomers in Heaven?

apart and destroy our witness as followers of Christ in the communities in which we serve. What if instead of trying to have the best youth group in town, we worked with the churches in our communities to make sure we were reaching every teen we could? Would that make a difference, even if another church ended up being the more powerful witness for youth? Could our identity issues and church ego accept that?

What is our purpose and goal? Are they aligned with His purpose and goals for our church and the communities we serve? Tough questions, but when we decided to follow Christ, I don't believe He says anywhere that it is about us. We are just the servants and imitators, called to follow humbly, without concern or regard for our positions or titles in this world. Our crowns come later, and if we can keep that in mind, I believe it will help us to maintain a steadier, not-so-flaky bearing in this life, no matter what comes our way.

The Great Attenders

It appears to me that the goal has been to see how many people we can get to attend our churches—or how we can fill up the local venue for a concert by a famous Christian band. Or maybe we bring in a special speaker and have him or her draw the crowd with dynamic presentations. Even on Sunday morning services, we love to count the attendees, like that really provides us with any real picture of our congregation and its capability to reach the community and make disciples. Unfortunately, I think it comes back to this whole emphasis on sponsoring events to make converts, but the issue as I see it is that making converts is one thing, but developing those conversions into followers of Christ is a lengthy and focused process that not enough of us are fully engaged in.

The professionals can't and shouldn't be the ones expected to do it. As I understand it, their role is to train up the laity to not only reach their communities but also mentor, model, and teach the basic foundations of the faith. If you are a lay person in your church, do you see this as your responsibility, and have you been open to training and development? Have you taken part in any spiritual gifting assessment or workshops that help identify where God has gifted you to serve in the body? Shouldn't this be

P J Anderson

included in our orientation and membership classes when we are going to make the commitment to serve in a local body?

Could you imagine the small groups we could establish to reach our communities as people stepped up to lead and develop others as they served? Or how about our youth leaders and children's ministry leaders being overwhelmed by the number of laity stepping forward to reach and teach the kids God has brought to our communities to be ministered to and discipled? Shouldn't this be the rule and not the exception? I am sure we have all heard the 80/20 rule, with 20 percent of the body doing the ministry, while the 80 percent looks on or makes excuses why they can't serve. Is it too late to change any of this now, or do we just shrug our shoulders and plug along? I think some of us are in for a big surprise when we stand before Him someday and try to justify why we sat on our hands and watched while the few faithful did their best to serve.

Lots of Talk—Few Results

It seems to me that we have placed a great emphasis on biblical knowledge and the level of degrees one can attain in our Christian colleges and institutions. Not to say we don't need solid teaching in our churches, but head knowledge and one's degrees of learning seem to be highly regarded. The actions of service and caring for the body as a whole, which we desperately need the body to be engaged in, are not given the same degree of emphasis or recognition as critical to the foundation of the church's witness and actions.

We offer many Bible studies and opportunities for members of our church to go deeper in the study of God's word. One common mind-set seems to be that if I attend church on Sunday and attend at least one Bible study, I am really healthy in my pursuit of God. Again the professionals are actually doing the ministry. I can be a passive participant, and this is normal. Oh, I almost forgot that if I post on social media, I get extra points for that as well. We know that is not what the scriptures teach us! Our biblical knowledge needs to be a part of our foundation for sure, but if our head knowledge does not translate into the body of Christ's actions of grace, mercy, and service, what do we have?

Are There Any Boomers in Heaven?

We have exactly what we should expect, a church that is shrinking at an incredibly fast pace, with the 20 percent of servants shrinking even more. This is only going to accelerate as we boomers keep aging and moving from our seats in the church to our seats on the front porch, transitioning from pew potatoes to windbreakers! I have personally seen a number of churches that have been converted to art museums or bed and breakfasts. One big one was converted to condos! I am sure we will have a lot to complain about—how the church isn't as full as it used to be and certainly not as dynamic, when we sat together and ran all our programs and had all our famous speakers come and fill us up even more. Really, that's what we will call success in our faithfulness as followers?

Generation NeXt

Generation X, which follows the boomers, is one that I am very concerned about. It is my understanding from the scriptures and throughout the church's history that each generation needs to build into the next generation and disciple them to become followers of Christ. I believe this is one of the biggest issues with my generation. We spent too much time trying to get the church to meet our concerns and establishing a model that we liked or found acceptable, and not enough of our spiritual energy went into reaching and developing the next generation. With a model that depends on the professionals and not the laity to make disciples, we have left a huge gap in our capability to reach and mentor as we have been instructed to do in the scriptures. There are just not enough professionals to do the job, and in reality, it is their job as leaders to train the disciple makers, not do all the work.

The reality is that discipling takes time, and building close relationships with those we intentionally want to impact takes a major effort on our part, not a passive, casual experience. I think a lot of my peers have felt they were not capable of taking part in any discipleship process, or worse, they were never provided with the teaching and modeling required to take on that role within the body. We can point fingers in both directions on that, but no matter how you approach it, the fact remains that boomers haven't had enough impact on the generation following them. We are seeing the

P J Anderson

results in churches today, with a significant reduction in the body as more boomers begin retirement and start moving out or are even less engaged.

Now we have the millennials coming into bloom. Are there mentors from generation X prepared to disciple them and fill the commitment needed to help them to grow deep in their faith? Based on my earlier position, I would say not enough have been provided with the depth to take on the level of responsibility and lack the kingdom-building skill required to fulfill that desperate need. One generation's lack of commitment and concern have multiplied and been passed on to the next. The Old Testament is filled with stories of the nation of Israel's generational issues. I think we can learn a lot about God's reaction in these situations, which should terrify us, first of all, and certainly make us think twice about our priorities for life as a generation of Christ followers. Am I focused on his expectations and priorities or on what makes me feel good and comfortable?

What Now?

Okay, enough complaints! Let's take some time to review what I see as some of the ways we can get our act together or at least focused on the right things. I know you may not agree with a number of my concerns and complaints. However, I think you would agree that there is a lot of ministry, discipleship, and mission work that we could be focusing on if we were all engaged and focused on kingdom work. I would like to look at some of the scriptural teaching and instruction that I see as pretty clear to help us to attain Christ-centered lives that are useful for the advancement of his kingdom wherever and whatever he chooses to use us for and for how long.

Go
SOLCA

In this section, I would like to suggest some key topics for you to consider and ponder, as I believe these are important areas to review and discuss

Are There Any Boomers in Heaven?

when I consider what needs to be addressed from both a personal and body life perspective. The title obviously does not make any sense, but for my purposes it outlines some very key areas that I believe we all need to consider in our quest to be followers of Christ and not just a cultural group with a Christian label attached. As part of this exercise, I am going to recommend various scriptures for you to review and ponder before you read my input on this topic. My prayer is that I will remain faithful to the message and intent of these passages as I present my input and challenge you to at least consider what I see as some key areas of the faith we all need to be immersed in to keep us on the right path.

CHAPTER 2

SUBMITTED SERVANT—
BEATITUDES MODEL
(Matt. 5:1–12)

Did you ever take time to consider the message that is provided for us within the Beatitudes that Jesus taught in His first major instruction to His disciples? Just the fact that it is His first teaching might give us an indication that this is something He wanted to say to us for a long time. Now He had the attention of those who would be His messengers, laying the groundwork for the witness that will be our primary guide for life until He returns one day. As I read these texts, I am trying to put my life and my decisions within the context of the instruction Jesus provided while remaining as simple and straightforward as I can, fully realizing that many more educated scholars have analyzed these text and may not see them in the way that I am proposing.

Poor in Spirit

In the first Beatitude, Jesus challenges us to be poor in spirit, with the promise of inheriting the kingdom of heaven. What does this really mean, and what does it look like? Simply put, I think Jesus expects us to come to Him with a spirit that is totally devoid of any self-centeredness, recognizing our poor, low position and total dependency on Him, fully realizing His kingdom can only be obtained from this perspective. Do we understand how poor we are?

Are There Any Boomers in Heaven?

Mourners

In the second Beatitude, Jesus tells us that we need to mourn to obtain any comfort. I know it has been asked, "Are we supposed to become professional mourners?" I am pretty sure this is not what Jesus had in mind when He said this, but it does speak to the position we should see ourselves in as we approach Him—extremely destitute to the level that we are mourning who we are and grieving our current situation in life without Him. Are we extremely sorrowful to the level of mourning our depravity?

Meek

In the third Beatitude, we are told that we need to be meek and our reward will be to inherit the earth. My assumption here is that He is addressing the new one that comes with the new heaven He will bring one day. The third position seems to really align with the two previous positions, first poor in spirit, then mourning our position, and finally to arrive at a position of total meekness. Put all of these together, and you have quite an image of what I would picture us looking like as we come to Him totally downtrodden and needy for something only He can provide! How low are we?

Hungry for Righteousness

This brings us amazingly to the next Beatitude, where it seems clear to me that Jesus is addressing the answer to our dilemma. But first He makes it very clear that if we are to seek His holy and perfect righteousness, not a self-oriented righteousness. We should seek this like someone who is desperate for food and water. It's interesting that He uses this analogy. As I think about it, if I don't ultimately get the food and water I need, I will die. In the same sense, if I don't receive His perfect righteousness, I will also die one day with no hope for the eternal life that He promised to those who would seek Him and as He promised, find Him. Are we hungry and thirsty?

P J Anderson

Merciful

Now that we have sought and received His righteousness, I believe we are positioned to look at these next Beatitudes from a different perspective. Would we really be capable of being truly merciful from the destitute, self-centered state we were in before we came to Him? I think the answer is clear—no way! But now that we have been transformed by His righteousness, we can begin to see life through a totally new lens—a lens with His filter in our being, now able to see things more clearly and from His perfect perspective and guidance. Now we are capable of being merciful to those around us and able to receive His mercy as a result. Are we His agents of mercy in this desperate world?

Pure Heart

Now we come to the real challenge in the Beatitudes as I see it. Who can say, save Christ, that they have totally pure hearts? I think those of us who are Christ followers realize that none of us have obtained this totally. However, He challenges us to seek this purity with the incredible result of seeing God. Jesus has the pure spirit, and we are provided with the Holy Spirit to fill us and to unite with our spirits to bring us as close as we can come to that in this life. Realistically, I believe Jesus wants us to seek this continually, fully realizing we won't obtain perfection in this life but knowing that we are totally dependent upon our submission to the workings of the Holy Spirit within us. Bottom line, we will continuously strive toward that perfect pure heart He wants us to attain. Are we totally depending on the ongoing work of the Holy Spirit within us to seek that pure heart He wants us to attain?

Peacemakers

Who would like to be called true sons of God? I sure would, and I would hope that most of us would. Let's face it, it is a real challenge trying to be a peacemaker in this hostile world we live in. Is there a day that goes by that we don't hear or see some crazy, hostile situation or sometimes are

Are There Any Boomers in Heaven?

the source of it ourselves? If we are going to truly be peacemakers, then I believe we are going to have to stand up for justice for those who are being abused or taken advantage of where we can have influence. This is where we have to be willing to stand up and take abuse from the powermongers, whether they are in our families, in the office, in the church, in politics, or in other cultures. Wherever these conflicts arise, we are to stand in the gap and try to bring about peace. That is one tough assignment, but He never said it would be easy. More to come on that as we go forward. Bottom line, do we seek to bring peace wherever we can?

Persecuted

It only gets deeper and more costly as we go, but the promise of seeing heaven one day, that makes it eternally satisfying. Surely none of us seeks out opportunities for persecution, but it clearly comes with the position if we truly accept it and understand the cost of being His follower. I am not talking about the rejection and scoffing you receive from family or coworkers once you become a follower of Christ. This is a bit more serious than that, and the results can be more devastating. If you doubt me, take a look at the cost our brothers and sisters face in the Middle East, China, or India—loss of family and shunned, abandoned, imprisoned, tortured, or killed. I believe this is what Jesus was addressing here, and we should not take this lightly because we haven't seen or experienced this degree of persecution here. We may be called to serve in a situation or location that is much more hostile and threatening than ours is currently. Things change quickly sometimes, so we all need to be prepared to stand up for Christ and willing to face the circumstances that come our way. Have you considered what you would do if you were faced with real persecution? Better question still, are you willing to stand up for and with your brothers and sisters who are being persecuted? If you are interested, you could ask World Relief, World Vision, Samaritan's Purse, Christian Aid, Voice of the Martyrs, or other organizations you might know about. Maybe your church is engaged in this somewhere, but in any case, we do have many resources available to us. We need to be paying attention. With the current refugee crisis in our faces, how can we ignore it?

P J Anderson

If my understanding is correct, our position requires that we come to Him poor in spirit, mourning our lowly position, with a meek attitude, hungering for the holy righteousness that only He can bring, which enables us to be merciful to others, seeking to be pure in heart, bringing peace wherever we go, fully expecting persecution for being His followers. It doesn't get any clearer than that for me. I see that as the challenge, and could we even imagine attaining any of His promises without having Christ and the power of the Holy Spirit at the very center of our lives?

CHAPTER 3

OBEDIENT FOLLOWER—FOLLOWING THE WELL-LIT PATHWAY

Now that we have addressed our position in Christ, I would like to look at how we are going to live that out in a consistent manner for the rest of our lives here on earth. How do we remain obedient within the most important relationship we have been provided with that will guide us to our eternal destination? The obvious answer that comes to mind is based on the promise Jesus presented to His disciples when He was preparing to return to heaven to be with His Father. That would be the wisdom and guidance that they and we would receive from the Holy Spirit. As a follower of Christ, it would seem abundantly clear that this would be necessary for us to sustain any kind of dependency and consistency in our efforts to be like Him. His model of obedience is the example we need to follow, and I would like to share some of the key principles He set that will provide a well-lit path for us.

Time with the Master
(Ps. 23, Prov. 3. 9:9, Matt. 14:23, Mark 1:35,
Luke 6:12, John 8:31–32, Matt. 11:28–29,
Luke 5:16, 18:1–8, 1 Thess. 5:16–24, Rom. 12:2)

This is very challenging, particularly for our culture, where noise of all types is normal it seems, even inside the church. We seem to have a need to have an abundance of noise or chatter going continuously. Could we

P J Anderson

really just sit in silence together, seeking His presence? Would that seem odd? Can we set our electronic devices aside for a while and just have that quiet time of contemplation that He has designed for us to enjoy when we truly seek Him with all our hearts? This is where obedience in following the well-lit path He has provided for us is necessary. We put that time aside because He has defined it as important to our understanding of His will for our lives. Continually seeking His wisdom, just like He did, will keep us on the path He has defined for us and allow us to find wholeness in Him.

We have an abundance of witnesses from the scriptures and church history recording the followers of Christ who have come before us who have experienced this and passed along their testimonies, which we can draw from as examples. The core witness for this is Christ Himself, as He would take the time in His hectic, sought-after life to be alone with His Father. Now if Christ our Lord built in time to be alone with His Father, how can we, His humble, lowly servants, do any less? He wants to spend time with us, and this is where we find real healing for the things that weigh on us deep in our souls.

This is also the time that we should invest in reading and studying God's word, which should become a consistent life source for us. Why do we need this? Hopefully the answer is to become more like Christ and not just to have a great deal of head knowledge. Really, if the word is not going to transform us, isn't it the same as any other book? We have been provided with many scriptures, which are a good witness for us to follow. You might even say as our guide, it is the journal that has been handed down for us to use as a source for wisdom and guidance as we navigate through this complex life. There are numerous models available to us, so there is no excuse for a lack of guidance and resources.

We can also apply contemplation and meditation. As we come to Him with a teachable spirit, we will experience that peace that is beyond our understanding. We also receive answers to the challenges we face in life. The scriptures are applicable for our circumstances and decision making if we are obedient to listen and follow the message provided for us. I can think back on the times I just went ahead with decisions my own and compare those to the times when I truly spent time with seeking His wisdom and guidance. Night and day, from walking in the dark to experiencing peace and a sense that I was walking in the light. Isn't that

Are There Any Boomers in Heaven?

what Jesus was doing in His set apart times of being with His Father to seek His will and gain understanding and direction for His life on earth? Here's a challenge: read a proverb a day for a month, and build in time to be quiet and meditate on those verses that stand out to you. I guarantee that you won't be disappointed, and you can use this as an example to work through other books in the Bible. Please don't take the most valuable resource you have been given in this life and set it aside.

If we are willing to build time into our lives, focusing on what He has to teach us in His word, meditating on what that means for us, our prayer lives will take on a whole different perspective. Rather than just coming with random concerns and requests, which may be appropriate at times, our prayers will now be integrated with His word as a guide with a focus centered more on His kingdom concerns than the more temporal things in life that we seem to get bogged down in. More time listening and less time talking. This is where the 80/20 rule might help. You should speak for 20 percent of the time and listen for 80 percent of the time.

Please ask yourself, "What would my prayer life look like if I was willing to put aside the mundane or wasted hours I spend on (you fill in the blank) and really had quality time alone with God, really seeking to listen and be obedient to the things that are important to Him and to join with Him to bring the kingdom of God to the earth? Fully understanding my position and the expectations He has for me, shouldn't that be the primary goal for life?" Bottom line, this is the most important appointment you have; don't miss it for anything.

Fasting is another one of those challenging topics that has certainly had a lot of questions and concerns raised on the purpose, method, timing, and relevance. However, we do have a cloud of witnesses on this practice, and Jesus's instruction seems pretty straightforward regarding His expectations for His followers. It seems abundantly clear that the practice of fasting has been aligned with prayer in the examples from the scriptures that have been provided from both the Old and New Testament witnesses. When people were seeking God's direction and wisdom on important concerns or issues, fasting was integrated with prayer. Should we do any less? I can only share my experience with this, as I have struggled at times to be consistent with this practice, but I will say that when I have been faithful, I have experienced that inner strength that takes me deeper in my awareness of

P J Anderson

His presence. He brings us to a deeper level, where we get built into in a way that is beyond our understanding.

One other thing that I would ask is that you do a little research on the benefits to our health that fasting can bring as well. If we view this from a holistic perspective, we will see that fasting has been included in our path for reasons beyond alignment with His will for our lives. It comes down to realizing that He knows what we need and what will bring us to not only spiritual but intellectual and physical health as well.

From the instruction provided in the Matthew text on this, we are certainly called to keep a low profile and not brag about our humble position, and God rewards those who come to Him in this way. This is obviously beyond our understanding and one of those areas of relationship that we may not see clearly now but hopefully will one day when we greet Him in the new kingdom. Rather than getting all legalistic or debating the hows and whys about this, shouldn't we just be obedient and follow the path provided?

Body Building
(1 John 1–9, James 5:16, John 4:23, Col. 3:16, Heb. 10:24–25, Matt. 28:19–20)

Now that we have focused our time and attention on our personal time and individual relationship with the Father, we see the path taking a different turn, which will require more interaction with our brothers and sisters, working together to serve Him and bring others into His kingdom. As we will see later, a lot of this will tie in with our spiritual gifting and the uniqueness we have been provided.

It is apparent from the gospels and the book of Acts that Jesus's method for developing His followers was not an individualistic model but one that requires interaction, accountabilities, and service to one another that is ingrained in everything He taught. This is so huge and important, but in the throes of our individual-oriented culture, it is hard to get the body to live this out with any consistency. In my experience, men are the biggest challenge in this. Anyone who has tried to develop a healthy men's ministry within a church will know what I am talking about. There are

Are There Any Boomers in Heaven?

so many conflicts for time and the willingness of men to go deeper and have accountabilities built into their life. On the other side of the equation, women are more socially oriented, but that doesn't mean that they are necessarily willing to go deep, which can add a whole different level of challenges for them.

The early church had its issues for sure, and we can read about many of the struggles they faced, particularly in Paul's letters, which always seem to be addressing concerns or weaknesses within a church body. That is not an excuse for us and we should be able to learn from their mistakes or miscues, which it seems obvious why we have them as examples to learn from and hopefully can gain some wisdom and insight from the teachings they provide.

Being part of a healthy body of followers of Christ should be obvious, but it seems to be one of the challenges we face today. Many don't trust the church or see its teaching as not aligned with the way they believe or question the motives. The battles regarding political correctness and where we stand on those issues seem to create even more strife and separation. My perspective is probably not going to be seen as favorable to many in the individualistic movement, but I am more concerned with being a Christ follower and trying to be obedient to His word on how we should live out our faith within the body.

Worshiping together as the body is one of those amazing experiences for me. We come focusing on our Lord and all the wonder and majesty of who He is, and somehow we come out with an incredible depth of blessing ourselves. It's another one of those mysteries of the faith that only He understands and allows us to experience when we stand before Him in humble admiration. When we look at worship, there are many different suggestions and ideas on what the best way might be to approach God— sometimes as a body, other times alone or maybe with a few.

All of these times are important, and taking the time to bring ourselves before Him is critical if we are going to make any efforts to step out and serve Him. Worship keeps us centered and focused on Him and what He has provided for us, and keeps us in our right place in service to His kingdom. I think this can get lost when we see a work being fruitful. We may place too much emphasis on our own accomplishments, forgetting the one who has empowered us and provides everything we need. We can

P J Anderson

become so full of ourselves that it becomes a detriment to the work He has called us to be faithful in following Him to complete. Is worship central and consistent in your life? Worship helps us to remain the servant and not the master, as our position remains clear and our empowerment is ongoing and consistent. Think about it this way: our study and learning combined with our silent meditation, prayer, and fasting prepare us to worship Him with all we have.

The personal forgiveness we receive when we confess our sins and submit to His cleansing sacrifice is central to our faith for sure, and only He can provide the release from that bondage of sin that we all need. We need to attain that holy righteousness that only He can provide. We also know that we will need to seek forgiveness and confess our sins to Him throughout our lives, as we are still sinners saved by grace, and that is needed every day of our lives. We are also called to confess our sins to one another and to forgive others' sins as well. This is where we need to have some deep spiritual relationships developed with brothers and sisters— those we can trust with confidence, who are able to handle our failings and weaknesses with love and caring. Where do we find that level of trust if we are casual attenders? Short answer—we don't! This goes back to my earlier discussion where I raised concerns about developing the body of Christ when we are all just casual acquaintances and not seriously growing together in the faith.

Growing this deep takes time and consistency in our walk together to the level of commitment that says, "I am going to be there for you in your darkest times, willing to listen to your failings without judgment." Do you have this depth of fellowship in your life? If we don't, based on what the word says, we are missing out on a key relationship that is needed in our walk with Him. To be willing to come alongside others and help them to find release from their bondages as we remain obedient to His word, supporting one another as true brothers and sisters in Christ. Isn't this the expectation He has for us?

What about our witness to others outside the body? Oh, I know a lot of people will say they don't have the gift of evangelism and somehow that releases us from any responsibility for reaching others with the love and grace of Christ. Unfortunately, this is an area of obedience that is ignored when we should all realize that all of us are provided with the basics and

Are There Any Boomers in Heaven?

understanding to reach others in a very simplistic way. True, you may not have the spiritual gift of evangelism, but we are all called to share our life-fulfilling relationship with Christ with whomever He may put in our path. We just need to pay attention to that still, small voice that is active in all of us. I fear that many of us are missing out on important appointments and relationships, even within our own families, by not following this well-lit path. Are we unwilling to share our faith with people when opportunities arise, fully understanding the wonderful lives that would lie before them, if they only knew our Savior?

Collectively, we provide a witness as well. How the world views us and our willingness to step out into our culture to serve Him there is essential for all of us to share. If we are only Sunday followers, what does that communicate? If they see us interactive with those in need in our communities and even willing to reach out to those in other countries, doesn't that say a lot about who we are and what our priorities are based on? Our collective actions of service as a body are, in my estimation, critical to the message we are delivering to our communities.

Managing Our Resources
(Matt. 6:19–21, 24, Luke 16:10–13, James 4:14–17)

Now it's time to get real personal! The use and management of our time, talent, and treasures are usually very challenging areas for discussion. People seem to shy away, unless someone is bragging about how much he or she has given to a work. We can see lots of discussion and concern related to this topic in the scriptures, which should highlight for us that these will be areas of challenge for us. The way I understand it, all of these come down to priorities in life. Some of us can't seem to find that quality time needed to serve faithfully, and others struggle with the how-much question on giving and to where. Some have excellent talents but are not fully engaged in using them or have not sought out opportunities or guidance to assist them in finding the right position to serve in the body.

Simplistically, this is where life and resource management need to be tied in with our faith walk. Setting the right priorities takes a lot of wisdom and guidance. On the financial side, there are good resources,

P J Anderson

such as Financial Peace, and I can't encourage you enough to engage in this or other similar models with others in the body. Money is a stressor and has ruined more marriages than almost any other issue from what I understand. We have to learn to manage it properly, if we think we will be able to provide resources for the most important work on earth: advancing His kingdom wherever He directs us. I participated in a program back in the early '90s, and it was one of the wisest decisions I ever made, both in helping me to get my financial life in order and preparing me to plan for retirement. Do you want to be able to serve Him in retirement or struggle to make ends meet? The freedom to serve well comes from living a disciplined life. Sounds like a contradiction, but think about this for a minute. When Jesus came to this world, did He just live a random lifestyle without regard for the expectations His Father set for Him? The answer is obvious, but aren't we called to be followers, seeking to find the path set for us by Him? Can we do that without His guidance and discipline? Not a chance!

Time is about creating a realistic schedule that integrates our time with Christ and service for the advancement of His work, fully utilizing the gifts and talents He has provided in a planned and consistent way. If we don't purposefully do this, time will leak away, and you will find yourself asking, "What did I do with the very limited time I have been given to serve Him?" Have you purposely looked at your time management to determine if you are out of balance or may not be able to serve because you have too many other things on your plate?

Our talents can be used in many ways, if we are open to spend some quality time reflecting on how we have been blessed and equipped. We should all be engaged in quality times of studying the scriptures, individually, in small groups, and within the context of the body we serve in. This provides the baseline guidance and understanding of the fundamentals of the faith we are to build our life journeys upon. From there we can assess our talents, with coaching from others if we need guidance, serving with all the skills and abilities we have been blessed with. If everyone in our church body were to fully utilize his or her talents, would it make a difference in our church's impact in serving our communities and providing an excellent witness?

Are There Any Boomers in Heaven?

All of these areas of our lives are challenging for sure, and we need to be obedient in seeking His wisdom and the support of our brothers and sisters in the faith so we can have an impact in serving fully without guilt or regret. When we serve Him freely with our time, talents, and treasures, there is an inner peace that transcends our understanding, and we experience a level of joy like no other.

A Blessed Joy
(Luke 4:18–19, 11:27–28, John 15:10–11, Gal. 5:22–23, Phil. 4:4, 8)

Think about it—when was the last time you really celebrated everything that He has done for us and the incredible future we will share with Him one day when we join Him in our eternal home? Following His path brings us to this final realization and the pure joy that we experience in knowing and serving Him. We get to celebrate now as a foretaste what we will experience one day when we join together with all His followers, family, friends, and the people we have always wanted to meet.

What is the purpose of our times of worship together? Do we come to submit ourselves to Christ's reign in our lives? Do we come to enjoy being in His presence together as His submitted followers, but also to experience that deep joy in our being that only He can bring? I believe that when we enjoy Him fully, we get to experience that blessed assurance He wants us to enjoy. His joy becomes our joy! We delight in Him and He fills us with His presence. What could be greater than that?

It really comes down to priorities. Do we want our kingdom and mansion now, or will we be willing to wait for the one that He has promised to those who remain faithful to Him? One of the challenges with this is that we don't really know what that all looks or feels like, but again we know we can trust in Christ and what He has promised. We need to focus on that and not our temporal concerns or what we can accumulate in this life. Are you truly joyful!

CHAPTER 4

LOVE CENTERED—THE MOST IMPORTANT COMMANDMENT AND A NEW COMMANDMENT

(Luke 10:25–28, John 13:34–35)

This Luke passage is portrayed differently in Matthew's gospel. I like the one in Luke better because Jesus gets the lawyer who knows the Old Testament to provide the answer that has already been given to them. From that perspective, I think it demonstrates how aligned Jesus is with the teachings of the OT and in a subtle way lets him know that he has the answer already. It's kind of like us. We have the answers all written down for us, but are we really paying attention and applying it to our lives? I am going to approach this text very differently from what others have shared for sure, but in pondering what it says, there is a lot that I would like to draw out and expound on.

All Our Hearts

We are first told to love God with all our hearts, and I would assume that when we think about what this means, our emotions come to mind. When we think about loving someone, we would naturally think about our hearts as the source of our love. But let me stretch this a bit to look at our hearts as also our life blood providers. Realistically, if our hearts stop pumping, our stories here are over, and I wonder if we ever think about loving our

God with hearts that we care for and keep healthy! It's with healthy hearts that we can love and serve Him best in these short lives that we have been given. I think we are to love Him with every portion of our hearts, the emotional and the physical, as we are to love Him with all our hearts. I am sure some are saying, "Are you serious?" Yes, I am. Let's press on.

All Our Minds

Next, we are told to love Him with all our minds, each of which has so many facets to it, left brain, right brain, control center for body functions, memory storage, input monitor, and so forth. So if we are to love Him with all our minds, there is a lot to consider—again, thought processing, keeping things in balance, and the like. I think one way we love Him here is to keep Him and His word at the center and use the intelligence He has blessed us with to be as effective as we can in impacting our world, whether it be research and science, medicine, social service, business, or serving in the church. If He is in the center our thoughts, efforts, and work in this world, it will reflect the deep love we have for Him and be an incredible witness wherever He places us. By using our minds to full capacity, and loving Him in all we can accomplish and bringing Him the glory, I believe we will be able to love Him fully in this area of our lives.

All Our Souls

Okay, now how do we love Him with all our souls? Looking at the soul as the current residence for one's spirit is the key here. This is where we have that incredible relationship with His Holy Spirit, which in this life is a mystery. For those of us who long for that and have experienced that peace down deep in our souls that only He can bring to us, we know His presence resides within us. That's a promise He makes, and we can rest assured He will make His presence known. So my short answer is that we love Him with all our souls by submitting our spirits to His perfect Holy Spirit, which radically changes us from the inside out! A mystery for sure, but one we can depend on.

P J Anderson

All Our Strength

Finally, we come to another difficult area to define as we ponder how to love Him with all our strength. Again, are we talking emotional, mental, or physical strength here? We don't have a clear answer unless we try to read into the text, so I am going to assume He means all areas. I think our emotional strength is demonstrated in the way we respond to and treat others. If we truly love Him in this area of our lives, then we will be mature in our care for others, not tearing people down or judging them, which is easy to do. We will have a strength of character that is evident to others, family, friends, coworkers, or even casual acquaintances. Bottom line, we are emotionally healthy.

Our mental strength can be demonstrated in pressing on to accomplish even the most difficult mental challenges, staying true to our deep-centered strength and knowledge that only He can provide. We know that our capacity for wisdom and knowledge is somewhat limited in this life, but we will use what He has given us to serve others and to bring His truth into our world wherever we can.

What about our physical strength? How do we love Him with all He has provided? I believe we have been blessed with a physical body that He expects us to manage and take care of, so we can serve Him through others. First of all, we have to care for our bodies, which means proper diet, exercise, sleep, and everything that goes along with that. How can we love Him totally with a body that has been abused and not cared for? We only get one, and I firmly believe we demonstrate our deep love and appreciation for what He has given us by caring for it and ultimately using our bodies to their full capacity. I think we need to realize the importance of this and make some adjustments where they are needed. Are we abusing His blessing or showing Him love with all our strength, which is necessary in serving Him in this life? What kind of witness do we present to others?

Now if we put all of these aspects of our being together and realize the expectation that God has for us in loving Him with all that we have been given, I think we can see how important this is to our relationship with Him. If we choose to ignore these or not make the true effort to be everything He has called us to be, do we love Him in the way He is calling

Are There Any Boomers in Heaven?

us to in this passage? "With all" and not just somewhat is what I see as the critical message here.

Neighbor as Self

This brings us to the second part of the scripture and another incredible challenge, to love our neighbor as ourselves. I find it interesting that the lawyer focused his question on this part, which led Jesus to share a key story to illustrate what that looks like. Looking at my input above, it's obvious that I would have had many more questions about the first part before addressing this one. I also find it interesting that whoever put the titles in for different sections of scripture titled this section "The story of the Good Samaritan." I know that was a key teaching for us and the lawyer in understanding our neighbor, but for me the primary teaching is the message on loving God with every aspect of our being. How can we even conceive of loving others as ourselves without a deep love for God as our foundation and source of strength?

We do have the story that Jesus presents to provide us some wisdom and guidance on what loving someone else as ourselves would look like for sure. The challenge, as I see it, is how do we apply this to our everyday life? What does this really look like? One way to approach this might be to take a risk and ask someone who knows you well how they perceive you. How do you treat others? When we ponder this question, do we see ourselves as genuinely concerned for others, or is it just part of the job? Can we see ourselves in this story? Am I the guy walking by, ignoring the downtrodden, or do I step in to see if I can help? What does the church in America look like, and what is our witness, here and globally? Are we pumping up head knowledge without practical sacrificial love at the core of our work? These are tough questions, but it's not me who is requiring an answer! Let's face it, there is nothing casual about being a follower of Christ. If we take this passage of scripture as outlining His expectation, we have a lot to be concerned with and need to be considering how we measure up when looking at this very challenging area of our lives.

27

P J Anderson

Love One Another
(John 13:34–35)

Now we come to another challenge regarding others we should love and a very important reason that goes along with it. In this passage Jesus is talking to His disciples and is apparently preparing them to live out their faith and witness after He is gone. With this new commandment regarding love, He brings a new level of challenge and expectation. Now that we love Him with all that we have and love our neighbor as ourselves, we need to really demonstrate our love for one another. With that comes a very important aspect of our witness to the world.

What is so amazing about this passage is that we see it lived out in the book of Acts, and the result of their genuine care and love for one another had a great witness to those around them. Tough question on this—is this what the world sees from us? Do they see a church body so loving and caring for one another that they can't help but be drawn in? I hate to keep harping on this, but the casual, weak commitment in the bodies of many of our churches is a sad representation of what we are supposed to look like. True love for one another comes at a price and a level of care that is not casual in any sense. Do we know our church family and love them the way He has called us to love them? Do we witness sacrifice for one another and meet the needs for one another? That's world-changing love, and from my perspective we have a long way to go.

Let's put these three aspects of love together. What a great witness we would be bringing to our communities and to the world if we could truly love the Lord with our hearts, minds, souls, and strength and love one another the way He has commanded us. Ultimately, we must love our neighbor as ourselves in a way that provides an incredible witness to the love and sacrifice He has made for all of us. We should invite them to share in the eternal joy we experience now and will celebrate with our Lord one day in eternity.

Paul's message to the Corinthians in 1:13 provides an additional clear message that has been passed onto us to provide further definition and attributes that we should be using as a resource for deeper understanding of what love is and is not from God's perspective. We can work very diligently and try to accomplish a lot, but it really comes down to our motivation

Are There Any Boomers in Heaven?

and priority. We should take some quality time and ponder this passage and question our reason for doing what we do when serving others. Have we attained the spiritual depth needed to love in the manner that Paul describes here? Is God's love at the center?

CHAPTER 5

CAREGIVER WITH PURPOSE— GIFTED FRUIT BEARERS

(John 15, Rom. 12, Eph. 4, 1 Cor. 12, 1 Pet. 4)

We have all been given some great gifts, and those gifts have been provided for a very important, no let me say, the most important work we will do while we are on this earth. Unfortunately, with our professional model for church, we have not spent enough spiritual direction and energy in focusing on this critically important task within the body of Christ. Not that guides and materials have not been written and made available for us to use. Generally speaking they have been ignored by too many of us. This is one of the major causes for the lack of growth within the church and also a hindrance to the healthy expansion of the church, as we have been called to live out our spiritual gifting in a unified biblical family context.

John 15 makes it perfectly clear that we are to become fruit bearers who will be lifeless branches if we were not connected to the vine that provides us with the life-giving power that indwells us. As Jesus makes it abundantly clear, we can do nothing without Him, and when we try, it is a man-centered disaster waiting to happen. This is where our understanding of the total dependency we have in Him is critical, and living out the spiritual disciplines keeps us on the right path. Now we will see how our spiritual giftedness ties in with our fruitfulness.

Hopefully you have taken the time to review the scriptures that outline our spiritual gifting. Again there are many training tools available to assist us in getting a deeper understanding of who we are and how God

Are There Any Boomers in Heaven?

has gifted us to serve Him in the body He has placed us to serve in. We need to make the effort to get connected and follow through. Chip Ingram's course "Your Divine Design" is a good training tool that you can use, and hopefully your church may have this or other similar training available for people to attend together, which adds that additional level of encouragement that we all need.

I think it is pretty clear from the scriptures related to this topic that the church is a body life experience and not a whole bunch of passive participants sitting around watching the few gifted do all the ministry. Again, our leaders should be overwhelmed with the abundance of volunteers stepping up to serve and be fruitful, fully utilizing the abundant gifting that God has provided the entire body through the power of the Holy Spirit. So the question remains for all of us. Are we going to submit to His will and serve Him and His church with the incredible spiritual gifts He has provided for us?

CHAPTER 6

ACTIVE IN FAITH—SERVING CHRIST AS FOOT WASHERS

(John 13:1–20, Matt. 20:25–28, 28:18–20, Mark 9:35)

This brings me to what I see as the logical result of all we have been discussing here. In the first passage I am referencing here, we see Jesus with His disciples as He is preparing to share the last meal with them. Jesus kind of sent them into shock, and Peter was really upset by Jesus taking on the lowest servant position by becoming a foot washer for all of them. I think we have to put ourselves in the room in that cultural context to really understand this. This was about as low as a servant could get, and if Jesus tried to wash my feet, I believe I could have quoted what Peter said and would have had a very similar reaction.

This position that Jesus placed Himself in was providing a hands-on example of what our position should be in our culture as well. Yes, we don't have foot washers now, but I believe we can grasp what that looks like and more importantly what our position should be. In the context of our church family, do we take the low servant position, or do we expect to be the one served? Am I looking at my brothers and sisters in Christ, willing to serve them wherever I can? Am I providing help in a healthy uplifting way, not creating dependency, which can happen easily in these situations? I have met some people in the body who seem to have grasped this important perspective, but it certainly is not the norm. Shouldn't it be? What an incredible witness we could be in this harsh, me, me, I

Are There Any Boomers in Heaven?

culture that we live in. I firmly believe we are to be a contradiction to our culture's norms!

If we are going to go out into our communities and call ourselves Christ followers who are active in our faith, what does that look like? What should the world see when they view the church body and its work? Do they see foot washers, willing to reach the lowest and the downtrodden in our culture and in other nations and ethnic groups, or do they see a self-centered, self-righteous people group, wanting to impose their beliefs on others? Obviously, we are to share our faith whenever and wherever we can but with dignity, respect, and the love we discussed earlier at the center of it all.

Now we come to the command Jesus provides in the last chapter of Matthew. This is a very explicit instruction and one of the most quoted texts in scripture, along with John 3:16. I think most of us can quote either of them without much difficulty. The way I see it, the key message is wrapped within two very important points that I think we should highlight and take into context when viewing this passage. It is very clear that we are to go, with the primary purpose being disciple making, with good and clearly defined instruction on what Christ sees as important.

What I see as the important context for this is the way Jesus wrapped Himself within the instruction. In the first part He lays out in detail that it is by His authority that we are to go, not by our authority, which brings a clear understanding of our position as message bearers. We are totally dependent on Him for all He brings to us in His power and authority first of all. Just to be sure we don't miss the point, He closes this passage with the clear message that we are not going alone. He will be with us to the very end of the age, and I believe that should give us some great comfort and reassurance that this is His work through us and not something we design or try to accomplish in our own strength. Could there be a greater position for us to be in than totally wrapped in His authority and with His in-dwelling Spirit to guide us and keep us on the right path? I think not!

Being active in the faith, following His lead and example, is not going to be easy by any stretch. From my perspective, in everything I have shared to this point, it seems clear to me that there is one great cost that comes to all of us. We have been given the free gift of salvation and all that brings, but are we willing to put Christ at the center and submit to

P J Anderson

His will for our lives? That is why I think it is important to look at who we are from a beatitude perspective to start with and seek Him along the path of obedience that has been laid out for us. This will bring us to the position of being open to the spiritual gifting He has provided for us, thus preparing us to become everything He designed us to be, centered in His perfect love at our core, in-dwelling us, so that we can see and love others in the same way He has demonstrated so clearly for us. I think we can become all He wants us to be and have the impact on future generations if we are willing to be followers of Christ with all that He provides for us.

CHAPTER 7

WHERE DO WE GO FROM HERE?

That depends on a number of things, but most importantly, are we seeking His will and direction to start with? Do we see ourselves on a well-lit path, or is it going to require a change in direction? Are we going to make the effort to discern His leading? Are there trusting brothers or sisters in Christ available who could help us or possibly provide some spiritual mentoring or direction for us? This would be a good place to start. I firmly believe that if we are truly seeking His will, He will reveal it to us, either directly in our time alone with Him or through a trusting brother or sister who may be able to see our gifts and walk with us as we grow in Him. From my experience, when He inspires us to move in a direction, we can also depend on Him to bring the right people in our lives to serve alongside and those who can encourage us if we are open and willing to submit to Him and those He brings.

There are so many needs both inside the body and in areas of ministry that the church should be serving and focusing on. I am going to highlight several. This is by no means an exhaustive list of opportunities, but hopefully this might bring some thoughts or ideas to consider. The obvious first place to start is in your area of spiritual giftedness. We will be most useful in the body when we are aligned with the way He has aligned the body to function, with Him at the center and the gifted servants connected and submitted to one another and united in His perfect harmony.

Grace and mercy are evident when we read the stories about Christ's life captured for us in the scriptures. The woman at the well, another who was about to be stoned for her sinful life, those who were blind, crippled,

35

P J Anderson

and even tax collectors were those whom Jesus spent a lot of His time caring for, lifting up, and ultimately teaching us what grace and mercy look like from a practical sense. Should the apple fall far from the tree? I hope the answer is obvious, but how do we become those ministers of grace and mercy in our culture today? Are there ways we can be a blessing to those around us, particularly the least of these? Have we as a church body focused our attention, efforts, and resources on the right people? Personally, I think we spend too many resources inside the church and not enough on missions and outreach opportunities to reach the most vulnerable. Let me state clearly that I believe we are to seek opportunities, develop plans, and expend resources that provide a hand up and not handouts, which from everything I've seen only creates dependencies. It's not an either/or situation; it's both/and. We need to develop the body for the strength it needs to serve and care for others inside the body, our local communities, and wherever He leads us out into the world. Isn't it obvious that in order for us to be able to do this, we need all hands on deck, not a few professionals and a handful of volunteers who are all overtaxed.

We need ministry staff and volunteers, teaching and leading our kids programs, developing our youth, ever expanding our community groups with lay leaders to reach our local areas for sure. We also need a dedicated staff and volunteers to reach out to communities or cities in our area where in many cases the most vulnerable in our culture live. Has the suburban church abandoned or not expended enough resources in this area? I think we are all challenged to assess that and see what percentage of our overall resources focus on these areas of ministry. Are we reaching into our prisons or youth lockups, transitioning the homeless, supporting abused women, connecting with foster kids? This is a huge area of ministry, and we won't do it on our own. This is where we need to partner with other likeminded church bodies and organizations if we are going to have significant impact. Prison Fellowship or Straight Ahead Ministries might be a couple of ministries to check out for partnerships, and I am sure there are some local organizations that are doing a lot in these areas for you or your church to come alongside.

Are you getting exhausted yet? Hope not, because we haven't even discussed the ethnic groups we are called to reach in places that have not had the opportunity to hear the gospel or partnerships we need to be

Are There Any Boomers in Heaven?

engaged in to expand the gospel in nations that are raising up indigenous staff and workers to reach their communities. Other opportunities through Christian micro-finance, medical missions, agriculture, animal husbandry, and many others are available to us. We need to step up and say, "Yes, we want to make a difference in the world, serving Christ wherever He leads us." You could contact World Relief, World Venture, Missions Door, Christian Aid, Samaritan's Purse, World Vision, Hope International, Peer Servants, or End Poverty, just to highlight a few organizations we can partner with. One final recommendation is that you subscribe to the *Missions Frontier Magazine* to keep abreast of what is happening in global missions, and if you want to go deeper, attend a local Perspectives Course.

When there are catastrophes, locally and globally, relief usually needs to be a first response, but that needs to transition to development, which should include the efforts of those impacted, hopefully leaving them in a long-term sustainable situation and the ability to grow forward. These tragedies seem to be incredible opportunities for the church body to demonstrate to the world what sacrificial love looks like—Christ's love with skin on, living out the faith in a way that is world changing. We have many refugee situations and need to be on the front lines here, not cowering to the fearmongers who would have us abandon our calling. Our Lord and His earthly parents were refugees when they escaped to Egypt. Something to think about.

I don't believe any of this is possible if we don't understand that as followers of Christ we all have a role to play in this kingdom work, whether serving in the local body, engaged in local outreach, or fulfilling a role in the global mission effort. We are all necessary, and those of us in the boomer generation need to step up and take the lead where we can and set the example for the generations coming behind us by mentoring, coaching, and providing opportunities for development or being a faithful servant. In my estimation, we are going to have a devastating impact on the church in America if we don't step up to serve where we are called. There is no going back once we've made the choice to expend our time, talent, and treasures on temporal things instead of serving to advance His kingdom.

CHAPTER 8

THE FINAL QUARTER— OUR LASTING LEGACY

I think I have offered enough challenges, and hopefully you will be willing to assess some areas of your life and see where you are and address some things that may need to change. No one can make that decision for us, but I believe the first step is being honest with ourselves about our priorities and focus. What do we expend most of our energy on? Is there a healthy balance in our lives? Some of us are already retired, but all of us will be coming to that crossroad soon enough. What will that look like? Is it time to check out or an opportunity to transition to an area of service or ministry that I couldn't do when I was employed full time? Let me be clear—from my perspective you may need some down time, a time for some silence and solitude, meditating on His word, and maybe seek guidance from trusted brothers and sisters.

What skills and gifts has God blessed me with? How can I apply those in this stage of my life? I firmly believe that if we will obediently follow the well-lit path provided for us, He will reveal the way forward. Those skills and gifts will become evident to you and to those who you will be aligned with to serve. Will there be sacrifice involved? Let's hope so! What about resources? Is it time to downsize or designate a portion of my retirement savings for investment in generating capital for the kingdom? We need wise counsel for sure and more time in silence and prayer as we prepare this aspect of our legacy as well.

Many of us raised children, and now a lot us are at the stage of enjoying grandchildren and watching them grow. What legacy and witness are we

38

Are There Any Boomers in Heaven?

leaving for them? When they think of us now and on into the future, will they remember us for our faithfulness and acts of service, sacrifices we made for others in serving our Lord? Are we examples for them to follow? This is an important part of our legacy, and we should not take it lightly, fully realizing that we may have a huge influence in helping them to set a direction in their lives. Do they know how important that Christ is in our lives? Have we discussed what it means to have Christ in the center of our lives? If Christ is truly not the center, won't it be obvious to them as they observe our lives? Is it toys, houses, money, or other temporal stuff that dominates our time, talent, and treasures, or do they see abundantly blessed fruit bearers, active in our service to Christ by serving others? Do they see dedicated followers of Christ, working to bring His kingdom, and not obsessed with maintaining our earthly kingdoms? Sorry for being so blunt, but there is no time for playing house with all these important people in our lives watching! Our life witness speaks volumes, and just because we show up at church every Sunday and park ourselves in the seat, does that really communicate anything significant? You certainly know what my opinion is by now.

The Book of Acts

We should all study the book of Acts individually and with others, as we can learn a lot regarding the formation of the church, particularly the way key individuals were built into by others. A very key learning from this regards mentoring and the importance it played in the early church, and I think it should be ingrained in every aspect of our ministry.

One character from the Bible that comes to mind for me in this stage of life is Barnabas. We see him in the book of Acts in a number of different positions and situations. When we first meet him, he seems to have gotten the resource issue in place, as he sells property and brings it to the leaders to be used for the work of the advancement of the kingdom. We should ponder that a bit, looking at our resources, and ask if there are decisions we should be making at this stage in our lives. Are there works or specific movements that you seem to have a kindred spirit with or may have experienced earlier on in life that you could be a resource for in this

39

P J Anderson

stage of your life? Examples might be street dwellers, prison ministry, microfinance for people living in poverty, refugees, people in transition, student ministries, preprimary schools, housing, and medical missions. The list certainly goes on, but I believe if you seek His guidance, the answer will come for you and will be aligned with how He has designed you to serve. I know I have made the statement about how resource rich our generation is, and I want us to recognize the huge opportunity He has provided for us all if we will pay attention to His leading.

We also see Barnabas as a mentor, particularly for Paul, this Christian persecutor who certainly earned the distrust of many in the church for obvious reasons. Why Barnabas? Was he more mature than others, and was he available to serve in this capacity? I think the answer is obvious, and he seemed to be a perfect fit for the position. First of all, I just mentioned two key aspects of his capability as a mentor. He was mature, and he was available. If someone comes into your fellowship and may need to have someone come alongside him or her, are you mature enough and is this important enough for you to have time available to work with the person? Sometimes we may have the opportunity to mentor a small group. Basic fellowship groups—or community groups, whatever you want to call them—should be the norm in every church body, and we need leaders to step up and serve. This is where we can build into others, possibly mentor a few, but more importantly be available for those coming behind us.

Could you facilitate a group on spiritual gifting or financial management or provide a marital seminar or support these efforts? Just a side note: it seems like marriages inside the church are failing at the same rate as those on outside—ugh! Families are devastated, and children always seem to pay the highest price. What's our role?

One other thought regarding Barnabas. We see the issue Paul had with John Mark as he saw this lack of commitment from John and wanted to set him aside. Barnabas, being the mature mentor, saw it differently and felt that he could work with him and restore him for future work in the kingdom. Here we see Barnabas mentoring Paul first of all, helping him to reach his full potential, and sharing with him in this incredible expansion of the church to the Gentiles. Now, he could have easily agreed to do what Paul was recommending, but I believe Barnabas was remaining true to his calling. Just as he took a crusty religious zealot and helped to mentor him

Are There Any Boomers in Heaven?

into being an effective leader in the church, he will come alongside John Mark and, serving as his mentor, help him to be restored and useful for kingdom work. And we know this is how the story ends, as we see Paul requesting John Mark to join him in the work later in his ministry.

Was Barnabas a generation ahead? I don't think we can determine that for sure, but we can be sure of his faithfulness and willingness to serve God in a very critical aspect of ministry that I dare say most of us could participate in at some level. It's obvious to me that this is how the church advanced, as we see the examples of Paul mentoring Timothy and Silas, to name a few. What about Priscilla and Aquila and the impact they had as a couple expanding God's kingdom in a house church model? These examples that have been set before us should be the norm, not the exception. How did we ever get so far off track? Hello, who are you mentoring! Sorry, I had to say it that way to make sure you didn't miss my point. I believe we will be remembered most for the time, talent, and treasure we spend on building up and building into others, not so much what we did personally. What we accomplish in life can have so much more meaning and impact for those coming behind us if we focus on those whom He has called us to serve and hopefully assist them in developing a deeper relationship with our Lord as they grow in Him.

What will our legacy look like, and how important is it? I think it is clear from my perspective that passing the torch should be central to our lives and the priorities we set. We have received an incredible free gift that Christ paid for on our behalf, and it seems abundantly clear to me that sharing that gift with others, so that they can share in that and experience freedom, is the most wonderful thing we can do in this life. Unless we take what we have been given and give it away, it doesn't really retain any value, does it?

It is my hope that this has been a challenge to you and hopefully will encourage you to not only go deeper in your faith but seek His will for how you will use all that you have been blessed with. Second, I hope to promote and develop harmony within the body of Christ's followers so that we can serve together to leave a lasting, healthy legacy for those generations coming behind us. If we can truly reflect the attributes of Christ, both individually and collectively as His body, then I believe our witness will have a meaningful, lasting impact, and if we don't!

P J Anderson

I purposely did not answer the question this book raised because it is obvious that it is not my decision to make. Our heavenly Father will separate the sheep from the goats, but Jesus Christ has provided both the model of His life and clear direction from the scriptures for us to follow. He gave us key commandments to center our lives on and a clear path to follow, which for me is a submitted, obedient, love-centered caregiver, who is active in the faith and building into the generations coming behind us. Providing a good witness and example for my family and friends, could my life be any more meaningful and fulfilling than that? I think not!

Printed in the United States
By Bookmasters